D1565712

Strong Leaders, Better Results:
Learn to Optimize Your Nonprofit Board

Advice from FUNdraising Good Times Columns

By Melvin B. Shaw, M.A.Ed.
and
Pearl D. Shaw, M.P.A., CFRE

First Printing - March 2020
Printed in the United States of America

Dedication

This book is dedicated to the men, women, and young people who commit their time, resources, and talents to the nonprofit organizations, institutions, and associations they believe in. Thank you for taking the time to make this world a better place.

We thank the newspapers and magazines across the country who bring our weekly column FUNdraising Good Times to their readers. Thank you to the Birmingham Times (Birmingham, AL), Black Business Ink Magazine (Winston-Salem, NC), Black Star News (NY, NY), Call & Post (Cleveland, OH), Cincinnati Herald (Cincinnati, OH), Denver Weekly News (Denver, CO), Houston Forward Times (Houston, TX), Insight News (Minneapolis, MN), Kansas City Globe (Kansas City, MO), Memphis Daily News (Memphis, TN), Minority Enterprise Advocate Magazine (Washington, DC/ Northern VA), North Star News (NJ), Pasadena Journal (Pasadena, CA), Richmond Pulse (CA), South Florida Times (Miami, FL), Tennessee Tribune (Nashville, TN), The Carolinian (Raleigh, NC), The East Texas Review (Longview, TX), The Michigan Banner (Saginaw, MI), The New Citizens Press (Lansing, MI), The Pensacola Voice (Pensacola, FL), The Savannah Tribune (Savannah, GA), The Weekly Challenger (St. Petersburg, FL), The West Side Gazette (Fort Lauderdale, FL), and Urban Views Weekly (Richmond, VA).

Thank you to all our clients who trust us to provide guidance as they grow their fundraising programs and campaigns. We appreciate your confidence and persistence.

Dr. Jan Young and Ms. Ernestine Berry at The Assisi Foundation of Memphis, Inc. have supported our work for years, sharing FUNdraising Good Times with the participants of the foundation's Before You Ask Class. Thank you both for your vision and the belief in our nonprofits!

Special thanks to Jill Keith and Sara Henneberger who have been a part of the FUNdraising Good Times team since we began writing our column in 2005. Our support throughout the years also includes Julie Christen, Sonya Garzouzi, Wendy Patterson, Gazelle Simmons, Pamela King, CJ Kirkland, and Amanda Fitzpatrick, who have helped bring our column and this book to life. As always, an eternal thank you to Eleanor Boswell Raine and Vernon Whitmore—formerly with The Globe Newspaper Group in Richmond, CA—for being the first to carry our column and to nurture our vision of sharing easy-to-read and easy-to-use guidance for those involved with nonprofit organizations.

Contents

About FUNdraising Good Times 1

Welcome! 3

Advice for Nonprofit Executives.. 5

Is Your Board Engaged? 7

How Diverse Is Your Board? 9

Evaluate Your Board from a Funder's Perspective...................... 11

(Re)Building Your Board Leadership, One Person at a Time 13

Create Your Fantasy Celebrity Board 15

Radical Thoughts on Nonprofit Boards 17

The Importance of Roles and Responsibilities............................ 19

How to Prepare for a Board Meeting as an Executive Director.... 23

Five Ways to De-Energize Your Board 27

Volunteer-Led Fundraising: It Starts with the Board................... 31

Ten Solutions for a Board Who Won't Fundraise......................... 33

How to Fundraise Without a Powerful Board 37

Don't Wait Until Everyone Resigns: How to Retain Board
Members and Staff.. 39

Advice for Board Members..**43**

Before You Say I Do 45

Are You On Board?..47

What Exactly Am I Supposed to Do?.................................49

How to Be a Successful Board Member............................51

You Can't Sell What You Don't Know 55

Key Duties of All Board Members....................................59

Six Simple Tasks to Energize Yourself and Your Board.............63

Board Responsibility for Financial Health 65

Fundraising Tips for Board Members 69

Combat Planned Confusion During Board Meetings.................73

Got a Minute for the Minutes? 75

Board Summer Refreshers..79

Supporting Interim Leadership..81

Replace Yourself, Sustain Your Board 83

What Will Be Your Fundraising Legacy? 85

Advice for All Nonprofit Leaders.................................**87**

Is Your Nonprofit Legit? Guidelines for Boards and Executives .89

Open, Honest Communication 93

Is Your Board Bored?...95

The Power of Nonprofit Volunteer Leadership 97

Building Consensus and Reaching Agreement 101

Should Board Members Give? 103

How to Increase Board Giving and Fundraising 105

Planning a Board Retreat...109

Assessing Last Year's Performance 113

Recommit to Fundraising 117

Tips to Achieving Fundraising Success 119

Three Powerful Fundraising Tools 121

About the Authors 123

About FUNdraising Good Times

In 2005 we started a weekly newspaper column filled with how-to information on the often-mysterious topic of fundraising. Our goal was to share our knowledge with those who manage, work for, or volunteer with nonprofit organizations, and help them attract and retain the resources needed for success. Our advice resonated with readers, and our reach gradually spread. Today our column appears in newspapers across the county and is also published as a blog at www.saadandshaw.com.

So who are Mel and Pearl Shaw? We're a husband-and-wife team with more than 60 years of combined experience in the fields of fundraising and marketing. We work with organizations and institutions across the country, advising them on strategic planning, capital campaigns, board development, donor relations, and much more. Many of our clients are historically black colleges or universities, some are churches, and others are local organizations, hospitals, foundations, and professional associations.

We see firsthand how nonprofits play a key role in our communities. They provide emergency services, educational and recreational programs, health care, legal services, job training, mentors, and more to generation after generation.

These organizations are staffed by employees and volunteers who are skilled, committed, and passionate about making a difference. Their board members are accomplished, well connected, and provide oversight, policy, and direction — often after the end of a long day at work. Their executive directors, presidents, and CEOs are visionary, talented, and often overworked.

We see these people all the time, and we know how vital they are to organizations. We also know the struggles they face to attract donors, secure major gifts, build a strong board, and create beneficial relationships, all while continuing to serve their community. We write our column for you.

We hope you enjoy this compilation of our columns.

Remember: Fundraising doesn't have to be drudgery — in fact, it can be fun!

Welcome!

We've compiled this collection of our FUNdraising Good Times columns and blog posts for you. Whether you're a nonprofit CEO/director or a board member, you'll find tips and guidance to improve your board's performance and ability to effectively fundraise. No matter what your role, we encourage you to read columns throughout this book to better understand the perspectives and needs of everyone involved, and to inspire positive change.

As we work with organizations across the country, we are frequently asked questions about boards.

What can I do to make my board more effective?

As a board member, how can I best serve my organization?

How can my staff support the board?

What role should the board play in fundraising?

This book shares our answers to these questions. It also shares information that will help your organization prepare to grow its fundraising.

For fundraising success, the board and staff must work together effectively. This can be a challenge for organizations of any size.

When expectations and goals are unclear, progress stalls, frustrations mount, and good leaders or board members may walk away. No matter what the state of your board, we offer actions you can take, starting today, to get back on track toward meeting your fundraising and organizational goals.

We want your organization to become known for the collaborative partnership between your board and executive leader. This collection can help guide your organization towards its ideal future – and towards an improved financial outlook.

The board plays a critical role in ensuring an organization's financial health and sustainability. Engaged boards are active in fundraising and take the lead in soliciting gifts, developing strategies, and supporting the work of staff and volunteers. Put the content of this collection to work as you invest in strengthening your board; your organization and community will thank you.

Mel Shaw and Pearl Shaw

Advice for Nonprofit Executives

Is Your Board Engaged?

Participation

In our decades of work with nonprofits we have worked with boards of all sizes, from large institutions to small grassroots organizations. We have worked with board presidents, members of development committees, and everything in between. This experience has taught us some valuable lessons about the crucial role of the board.

Here's one key lesson: All organizations benefit from having an *engaged* board. When your board is engaged it sets a tone and direction that is inspiring to all members of the organization.

Engaged board members attend meetings and show up prepared and on time. They serve as advocates for the institution, sharing their knowledge of its vision, mission, activities, future directions, and impact. They understand the challenges facing the institution and are creative in helping find solutions and attract resources. They are team members who respect each other and are willing to check their egos at the door. The good of the institution is paramount.

As team members, they are willing to roll up their sleeves and help make things happen. They are accessible and willing to partner with the executive director and staff members, volunteers, donors, and funders to create solutions that help the organization deliver on its mission.

Engaged board members welcome transparency and accountability and understand the need for honesty and policies that guard against conflicts of interest. They commit — as a collective body — to raising a meaningful percentage of the organization's budget. Each member makes a significant gift to the organization (in relation to income, assets, and connections).

Engaged committee chairs convene their committees and ensure goals and activities tie to the organization's larger strategic direction. Those committees encourage participation by individuals from outside the board who can contribute expertise, skills, and resources. Committee reports are distributed prior to each board meeting so members can read them in advance.

Engaged board members are proactive in identifying opportunities and in alerting each other — and staff — to potential challenges. When they have questions, they ask them. If they feel the organization is not headed in the right direction, they encourage thoughtful discussion. When they learn of developments in the field that could impact the organization, they share the information. When an outside perspective could help, they suggest consultants, workshops, or a visit from the leader of a comparable organization.

When we hear an executive director say, "My board supports me 100 percent," our ears perk up. We wonder, is that a good thing? A board that questions and encourages additional ways of looking at a situation can contribute to organizational health. When a board rubber-stamps the work of an executive director it may be a signal that board members are not engaged. Take a look at your board — what do you see?

First published October 17, 2011.

How Diverse Is Your Board?

The board of directors of a nonprofit organization is responsible for the organization's financial health. The board is also charged with hiring and evaluating the executive director, creating policies and procedures that guide the work of board and staff, articulating the organization's mission and vision, and ensuring the organization has access to the funds it needs to deliver on its mission.

But who are these board members? Who is making decisions for the organizations we rely on and are engaged with? If you are a member of a church or other religious organization, attend or work at a community college, seek food from a food bank, visit a museum, ride the bus, or visit a hospital, you are interacting with a nonprofit organization. And each is governed by a board of directors. They are making decisions that impact which services are offered, how donated funds are used, which government grants are pursued, and ultimately how these organizations will help — or not help — individuals, families, and communities.

Board members who govern public agencies such as transit authorities and community colleges are elected. Others such as board members of faith-based organizations, private colleges, and grassroots organizations are selected by people who are already sitting on the board. Still others are elected by members of the organization. This is true of membership organizations such as the Sierra Club.

The composition of the board is increasingly important to funders, donors, staff, and the very people served by an organization. But what is diversity? The San Francisco Foundation holds diversity as a core value that guides its work. They define diversity as "the range and variety of characteristics and beliefs of individuals that encompasses, but is not limited to, race, ethnicity, gender, gender identity, sexual orientation, disability, age, economic class, immigration status, and religious belief."

Here is our question for your organization: How do you balance your board's membership? How do you ensure your board represents the people you serve? That it also includes people with access to wealth and decision-makers? Do you engage individuals who can provide guidance in the areas of financial management, fundraising, personnel, and emerging trends in your content area? Are your board members required to conform to a specific viewpoint? Is agreeing with the board chair or executive director a requirement for membership?

Each organization answers these questions differently. How does your organization give life to diversity?

First published May 31, 2009.

Evaluate Your Board from a Funder's Perspective

Preparation

Donors and funders don't necessarily tell you why they won't fund your nonprofit. Many will make their evaluation based on your organization's presentation and reputation without sharing their objections. But if you know the criteria by which you will be judged, you can proactively prepare.

We recently had a candid conversation with corporate representatives to learn what they look for when investing in a nonprofit. Not surprisingly, the conversation started and ended with a focus on the role of the board of directors. Funders assess the board in determining whether or not to give, and the level at which they will give. That assessment includes a look for corporate representation. They want to know who is on the board, how they are involved, what they collectively give, and how much they raise. They look at small cues that communicate an organization's capacity and board engagement. Who circulates throughout the community with the executive director? Is he or she accompanied by other board members or senior staff when attending meetings or events? Do board members identify themselves as such when they circulate personally and professionally?

The funders we talked with see the board as the party responsible for sustaining and growing a nonprofit. They want to know if the board can provide the resources and funding to grow the organization, with or without the executive director. They won't invest in nonprofits where the board does not demonstrate the leadership required to guarantee growth. Having a strong executive is not enough.

Related to current board involvement is the issue of "the bench." Funders want to know how the current board is engaging and cultivating future board members. For community-based organizations, the questions relate to the process of growing from a community board to a diverse board that integrates, welcomes, and engages professionals and corporate representatives. Those we talked with mentioned the importance of boards knowing what type of leadership model they seek to emulate.

While concerned about funding for today, these funders are equally focused on an organization's ability to succeed in future years. They want to know about succession planning. Who is capable of ensuring continuity of operations should the executive abruptly leave? They want to know if and how the board surrounds the executive director with professionals who can help attract people and resources. Finally, they made it clear that they invest in nonprofits where their employees provide board leadership. Funding and resources follow employee board engagement.

The bar is set very high. But you can't meet the mark if you don't know what it is. If you have been struggling to grow your organization to a new level of operations, and are seeking corporate support, you may want to consider looking at your nonprofit from the perspective of a corporate funder. What will they see?

First published July 22, 2013.

(Re)Building Your Board Leadership, One Person at a Time

What do you do if you are a nonprofit executive director or board chair and you know in your heart of hearts that your current board can't do what needs to be done? We have observed a tendency toward several responses. One is to bury your head in the sand and hope the situation improves, another is to hope your term ends before the situation gets too messy, and another is to swear, "I'll fire them all." We have another way: Find one right person.

You want to find one person who understands and believes in your vision and mission. Think of who you know and start there. This is an interview process of sorts. You want to interview them, and you want them to interview you. You need to get to know each other. Do you share common values? How do each of you think? Do you understand each other? Can you create an open line of communication that includes trust?

Be open and honest. Share your strengths, challenges, weaknesses, and the opportunities that lie before you. Don't paint an unreal rosy picture. You want someone who can complement your strengths, help find ways to address challenges, and identify areas where you need professional development. You won't know if you are talking to the "right person" if you're not honest.

You need a person who shares the same vision and values that you do. But you don't want a clone of you — you want someone with experience, resources, and contacts that can help your organization grow to the next level. You want to extend your circle and increase your knowledge and resources.

This is not a "task" to be delegated. Don't depend on others to find your leadership! If you do this, you will find yourself with leadership that others are comfortable with, but who may not be the right fit for you. Don't farm this out. You don't have anything more important to do! If you can't attract one person, how can you attract and build a new board?

Don't be pressured by funding agencies and other outside groups to "do something about your board" immediately. If your board is dysfunctional, or the organization needs access to different perspectives, skills, and relationships, the change won't happen overnight. This is a growth process. You will need to let the people who provide funding and influence know that you want to take your time and find the right people — one person at a time. Don't try to build your board by Friday. You may find yourself locked into a nightmare.

Before you ask someone to serve on your board, ask them to work with you as an adviser. Over time, your advisers may become board members. Or they may provide the advice you need to bring out the best in the board you already have.

First published March 19, 2018.

Create Your Fantasy Celebrity Board

If you could have any five celebrities on your nonprofit board, who would you pick?

Visualize yourself as chair of the board of a nonprofit you believe in. Maybe it's a university, an early childhood education center, a food bank, international research institute, or performing arts company. You pick the nonprofit <u>and</u> the board members!

Focus first on your vision. As board chair, what do you want the organization or institution to accomplish under your leadership? Be specific. Do you want to ensure all first-year college students graduate in less than five years with less than $12,000 in student loan debt? As an early childhood education program, are you seeking to enroll 97 percent of children under age five years of age within a two-mile radius? Do you need to fully automate the warehouse for the regional food bank? Maybe you want your research institute to bring two new drugs to clinical trial. As a performing arts company, do you seek to increase the number and quality of performances? You determine your vision, and then pick your board.

Make a quick list. Does it include Sheryl Sandberg, Malala Yousafzai, George Lucas, and Melissa Harris Perry? Are Sean Hannity, Whoopi Goldberg, or Mark Zuckerberg on your list? What about Kim Kardashian, Lorretta Lynch, and Jon Stewart? Or maybe you are thinking of Serena Williams, Beyoncé, Joel Osteen, Ellen DeGeneres, and Michelle Obama. You have a universe of celebrities to pick from!

Review your list with an eye to the qualities "your" celebrities possess. Look beyond the obvious "rich and famous." In fact, don't consider wealth and fame. Think about what attracts you to each celebrity. Is it their creativity, persistence, sense of justice, risk-taking?

Remember to focus on your vision. Which celebrities possess the qualities, experience, and connections that can bring your vision to life? Are they accessible? Committed to a personal or public vision that dovetails with yours? Are they passionate about it? Do they have access to people who can bring your vision to life? Do they follow through on their promises? Are they willing to be an advocate? Can they move beyond their "celebrity" to let a cause be the focus? Are they respected? Do they have political connections, influence, a proven track record? Are they involved with other nonprofits?

Once you have your top five, it's time to determine how to approach each. Remember, this is your fantasy board — there are no barriers standing in your way. So, what will you say? How will you make your case? What do you want your celebrities to actually do as board members?

Now, back to reality. Can you think of people in your community who can help you bring your vision to life? Who will you pursue and why? The choice is yours.

First published May 11, 2015.

Radical Thoughts on Nonprofit Boards

"How many of your current board members are actually worth paying? If you had to pay your members, what board positions would you fund?" These questions caught our eye as we read a promotional piece for a book about philanthropy.

The author, Jimmy LaRose, poses some provocative thoughts in his book *Re-Imagining Philanthropy*. He promotes the idea that boards are not about governance, visioning, policy-making, volunteerism, or management. He believes these roles should be filled by a strong CEO. He advocates for a board of six experts who cover the areas of law, communications and marketing, entrepreneurship, and accounting. They should be joined by an expert in your area of programming and a nonprofit expert. That's it! Their role, in LaRose's opinion, is to fulfill obligations related to IRS compliance. The rest of the roles attributed to board members, he believes, can be filled by advisers.

Reading the promo piece triggered a major question for us: How would an executive director and staff prepare for a board meeting knowing that board members were being paid $1,000 per day plus travel expenses (LaRose's idea). How would the board chair and the board members prepare? Would the level of preparation required by all parties increase? What items would be on the agenda? How would the time be used during the meeting, and what type of follow-up would occur?

Would you pay your board members to attend a board meeting? Would you pay them to participate in a teleconference? What would you expect in return? Are your expectations tied to compensating board members for their time? Are you uncomfortable asking board members to bring their expertise to the table without pay? If yes, why do you feel that way? If you are a board member, do you treat your board responsibilities differently from your professional obligations? Do you bring your "A game" to board meetings?

Here are a few other questions. Do you believe the board should determine the vision, or should that be decided by the executive? In general terms, do you operate with a strong executive or a strong board? Who is setting direction for your institution or organization? Does it make a difference?

In our experience, the relationship between the board and the executive is an important one. We believe that ideally power should be shared, with accountability and transparency as core values. Related to this, we know that many small colleges and grassroots organizations face challenges related to sustainability. The suggestions made by LaRose are not necessarily the right remedy, but we also know that many organizations don't have the right balance between the executive and board. At times each party points the finger at the other, and too often neither one has the ability to secure the resources required for excellence. What are your thoughts? What is the way forward?

Disclaimer: We haven't read *Re-Imagining Philanthropy* and are not endorsing it.

First published August 14, 2017.

The Importance of Roles and Responsibilities

A great idea can be the first step in the process of creating something wonderful. Bringing the right people together adds power to the idea. Having roles and responsibilities to guide the work can turn possibility into reality.

If you want your idea to grow, be deliberate about who you invite to join your board. Think about what you are trying to achieve and what it might take to get there. Consider who has the required skills, resources, creativity, and connections. Make a list. Know why you are inviting people and what you want from them. Be prepared for ideas, suggestions, and leadership you may not have anticipated.

Write down the role and responsibilities you want each person to claim. Share your list with potential team members as you invite their participation. This lets people know what you are looking for, what you want them to do, what they can expect, and how they can best contribute. This can also establish norms for the group and help make sure you and your team don't get overwhelmed or sidetracked.

When inviting people to work with you, be prepared for them to suggest a role — or to take on a responsibility — you may not have imagined. That can be a good thing and it can moderate the feeling that you are "boxing people in" with roles and responsibilities. You want people to bring their best game, to know you have thought through a meaningful role for them to play, and to experience a structure that supports their highest level of participation.

Think about it this way: You bring the right people together. They are busy turning your idea upside down, creating solutions, envisioning partnerships, and identifying resources and connections they can contribute. They spend hours thinking through the ins and outs of your idea and have an initial blueprint for how to proceed. At the end of the process, they learn that their thoughts are appreciated as input, but someone else (not in the room!) will decide how to roll out the idea. If your group members were participating with the understanding that you wanted their best thinking, they may feel they wasted their time.

14 ways that roles and responsibilities can positively impact your organization and board:

1. People know how often they are required to meet, or if they will be asked to meet at all.
2. They know whether or not they are asked to give money or ask others for money.
3. They know how decisions will be made. This could be by consensus, a vote, or by another means.
4. Each person understands what you want them to do.
5. They understand why they were invited to be a part of the group.
6. They understand what you are seeking to achieve.
7. They understand who has organizational "power" within the group.

8. People know what they can expect from each other, and what they should expect from themselves as a group.

9. Tasks are not duplicated.

10. Tasks are completed on time.

11. Time is used appropriately.

12. Progress can be made toward agreed-upon goals.

13. Participants know who is responsible for what.

14. Expectations can be raised or lowered.

A few final things to consider:

1. Finalize agreed-upon roles and responsibilities in writing to help avoid misunderstandings.

2. Share everyone's roles and responsibilities with the full team so each person knows the role of each team member.

3. Build in incentives, acknowledgement, and recognition that communicates your appreciation.

Talented, creative, and connected people can help birth or grow an idea and expand its potential. The type of people you bring together — along with defined roles and responsibilities — will define how, when, and if the idea takes root.

First published June 10, 2018.

How to Prepare for a Board Meeting as an Executive Director

The board of directors plays a critical role in the life of a nonprofit. While each board is unique, best practices can increase a board's effectiveness. To learn more, we talked with nonprofit consultant Kim Moss. His leadership helps boards increase their capacity for governing and fundraising. We asked Moss for recommendations regarding how often boards should meet, and why.

He responded, "It is my experience that nonprofit boards are best served by meeting monthly. I have had experience with agency boards that only met quarterly and found that the majority of the problematic issues being faced by the organizations could have been avoided if the board had met monthly to keep up to date on the business of the organization. Monthly meetings allow members to remain updated about the finances and all other important aspects of the agency. The board is the greatest asset that an executive director has, and keeping them engaged is always beneficial to everyone."

Most importantly, board members must come to meetings prepared. We asked Moss what specific information an executive director should provide to the board. He focused on five areas, noting that while the executive director may not be responsible for completing each of these tasks, he/she should ensure they are completed. *All materials should be distributed to board members a week in advance so there is time to review.*

1. **Minutes.** These include minutes of the previous board meeting and minutes from board committees (fundraising, program, board development, audit, etc.) that met prior to the upcoming board meeting. The committees are responsible for taking minutes; the executive director should ensure all minutes are distributed.

2. **Meeting agenda.** The board chair should create and distribute the agenda for the upcoming board meeting. The executive director should assist if necessary.

3. **Financial statements.** The executive director should ensure the treasurer has the prior month's financial statements before the finance committee meeting. The treasurer will present the financials to the committee for review and, upon committee approval, will send them to the entire board.

4. **Executive director's report.** This should provide an overview of the agency's activities since the last board meeting, highlighting successes and challenges. Moss suggests the manager of each agency program submit a report that includes information about the number of people served, and an update on the program's scope of services.

5. **Grants management report.** This should document spending of grant funds on a monthly basis, the cumulative amount spent to date, and the amount left to be spent in the contract period. It is easy for an organization to get off track with spending. Overspending can be detrimental to the agency's financial health, and underspending on a contract signals to funders that funds are not really needed or are being poorly managed.

The bottom line? Board members need a clear understanding of the agency's financial, programmatic, contractual, and fundraising activities, and enough information to provide meaningful oversight.

First published September 5, 2016.

Five Ways to De- Energize Your Board

There is an ideal board in the consciousness of many nonprofit leaders. It often involves members who are engaged in governance and fundraising, who advocate for the organization, and who serve as community ambassadors building relationships and partnerships. These ideal board members are well-connected with time to spare. They magically appear, need no support or attention, and easily attract other like-minded people.

In reality, too many nonprofit boards are far from this ideal. The directors who report to these boards are pulled in many directions, are forced to wear many hats, and struggle with too much to do and too few resources. Building and sustaining an engaged board is another item on a never-ending to-do list. It's one of many items that are moved to "next week."

The dream of an ideal board co-exists with actions that will eventually de-energize even the most engaged board. While energizing your board will require time and attention, we can offer an easier alternative: five ways to de-energize your board. As you can imagine, many of these are easy to implement.

1. **Fail to communicate.** There are many ways to accomplish this. Change the date and time of the board meeting, and change it often, with little notice. Present inaccurate data with information that is confusing and with internal inconsistencies. Send materials to board members at the last minute. Send them by email with 10 different attachments that need to be opened individually.

2. **Fail to resolve issues as they arise.** Continue discussion on low-priority items for several months. Contribute to ongoing "issues" by being evasive and inaccessible. Don't worry about distributing minutes and reports in a timely manner. Don't proofread materials.

3. **Ignore suggestions and offers of assistance provided by board members.** Let them bring up their ideas meeting after meeting. Eventually they will stop. Prohibit staff from following up with board members, and actively discourage initiatives that board members want to organize independently.

4. **Use the same agenda for each meeting, and keep it full of reports from staff.** Don't allow time for board members to engage and provide input. Don't let the board chair create the agenda, set meeting dates, or set goals for board involvement. Don't meet with the chair between meetings.

5. **Recruit community leaders and then ignore their capabilities and connections.** Stay busy so you don't have time to learn the resources and funding that board members can give, raise, or attract. Fail to plan and then ask for help at the last minute when the timeframe is unrealistic, and the chances of success are slim. Increase the likelihood of disillusionment by failing to define goals, roles, and responsibilities. And when you do define these, do it on your own without consulting the board. Don't collaborate.

These are five ways to ensure poor attendance, boring meetings, and a de-energized board. It doesn't have to be this way, but you will have to do something to change the situation. Ideally, you will take action with your board. Together you can reenergize.

First published April 17, 2017.

Volunteer-Led Fundraising: It Starts with the Board

Volunteers

How do you develop a volunteer-led fundraising program? It's not something that happens overnight. It begins with the board and the process of creating an awareness of their fundraising-related roles and responsibilities.

If you are a staff person, here's one way to start engaging your board—meet individually with each member to share an overview of the organization's fundraising priorities and how these tie to its mission and vision, as well as to daily operations and budgeting. Share where the money comes from. How much comes from foundation grants? From government grants? Get specific. For example, share how many $5,000 gifts the organization hopes to receive this year. How many $50,000 grants? How could changes to state or federal budgets impact expected funding? Let each board member gain an understanding of revenue sources.

During these one-on-one meetings, ask each board member how they feel they can contribute. There are many roles a board member can play. They can work on the special events committee, meet with elected representatives, host friend-raisers at their home or office, help redesign marketing materials, create a social media presence, proofread proposals, speak with the leadership of their faith organization to explore the possibility of a gift, write an op-ed piece, secure pro-bono legal services, and of course, write a check and ask others to do the same.

Your job is to ask for suggestions and ideas. And to listen.

After completing these individual meetings, update the organization's formal fundraising plan with information and ideas you have gained. If you don't have a plan, create one. If you don't know how to create one, contact us and we can send you guidelines. Once your plan is up to date, share the plan with the full board. Let board members talk about what they are planning to do. Let them make their commitments to each other. After the meeting, make more adjustments to the plan to reflect the discussion of the full board. And then partner with your board chair — or chair of the development committee — to work with board members as they fulfill their commitments.

Once board members start to get engaged, staff can partner with them to begin the process of securing volunteers from outside the organization.

First published June 13, 2011.

Ten Solutions for a Board Who Won't Fundraise

What do you do if your board doesn't have the connections, experience, or willingness to be involved in fundraising? How will your nonprofit secure the money and resources it needs to deliver on its mission?

We encourage board-led fundraising. We believe that when board members are actively involved in fundraising, the nonprofit organization or institution will be more successful. Board-led fundraising includes active involvement in determining fundraising goals; identifying, cultivating, soliciting, and stewarding donors; making a gift of their own; and engaging others in giving and fundraising.

But what if your board is reluctant to fundraise or simply refuses to "give and get"? There are many reasons for this response. Members may not have been recruited to fundraise. They may be engaged in campaigns for other nonprofits. They may not know how to provide guidance and direction as it relates to fundraising.

If you find yourself in this position, **here are 10 things you can do as a nonprofit executive:**

1. Appeal to your board to increase their participation in fundraising in spite of original board responsibilities that might not include fundraising.

2. Visit each board member individually to learn more about the "hidden gems" — those ways an individual board member could be of service, or the reasons for reluctance to fundraise.

3. Take your board on field trips to observe other nonprofit boards in action.

4. Ask board members to recruit someone they know who has experience fundraising to work with each as a partner. Working in teams with colleagues from outside the board can build capacity and expertise.

5. Develop an alternative fundraising group such as a development taskforce, advisory council, special development committee of the board, or friends committee. These are people who can open doors, solicit, and provide guidance and strategy. They should be recruited with an explicit request to assist with fundraising.

6. Hire a consultant to work with the board to help increase their knowledge of fundraising responsibilities and ability to participate in fundraising.

7. Assume more responsibility for fundraising. You and your staff will have to be more active and proactive.

8. Scale your fundraising needs/goals to meet the capacity of board members and staff.

9. Work with board members to determine which fundraising projects they could take the lead on. This can help build experience and confidence and hopefully increase their appetite for more involvement. Don't involve board members in a big project they don't have the capacity or experience to achieve.

10. Keep the board informed on a consistent basis regarding the status of fundraising, funds received, prospective donors identified, potential shortfalls or surpluses, and the implications.

We live in an imperfect world. Work with your board, recognize their strengths, and offset their challenges.

First published September 7, 2015.

How to Fundraise Without a Powerful Board

Teamwork

What if your nonprofit isn't comprised of people with power, wealth, and influence? What if your board chair can't pick up the phone and raise $1 million? How do you compete when you feel other organizations are supported by power-brokers and you can't get your message heard?

Use the assets available to you. Build a team and relationships that will serve you for the long run. You may be surprised by the resources and riches available within your network. Here are some suggestions to consider.

First, remember it's hard to raise money from behind a desk. You have to be constantly out in the community making the case for your organization or institution and developing relationships. This is your work as CEO. It's also the work of board members and your development director or vice president. Get the pulse of your community and find ways to implement your vision in partnership with others. Take names! Build your list of contacts. Stay in contact. Don't depend on social media for your communication — build and nurture mutual relationships.

Consistently grow your list of prospective donors. If you need to raise $250,000 we recommend creating a list of people, businesses, foundations, and granting agencies who can give a combined total of $750,000. You don't have the luxury of assuming people will give the amount you request. You need enough prospective donors to cover the reality that not everyone gives. Even if you think it is a sure deal, make sure you have a plan B.

Talk with your staff, advisers, board members, and friends. Ask them who they know and who they can influence. It's not only high-profile people who can open doors! You don't know who knows who — if you don't ask, you may be missing an opportunity. For example, our experience has shown that barbers, hairstylists, maids, waiters, and waitresses have the pulse of a community.

Keep it personal. If there is someone within your organization who knows a donor or volunteer, ask them to take the time to personally thank those who give their time and money.

Always debrief with your development director. Let her know who you are visiting. Make sure contact information for those you meet is entered in your database. Don't assume you are the only person with relationships. Ask team members for suggestions before going into a "big meeting."

Become politically astute. Know your government leaders and make sure they know you and the priorities of your organization.

You may feel frustrated that your board or staff need to "catch up" with you. Don't let that get you down. It is your responsibility to communicate with passion and vision, set direction, and invite others to join you.

First published September 14, 2015.

Don't Wait Until Everyone Resigns: How to Retain Board Members and Staff

Retain

"Nobody taught us how to go out and fundraise." — Former board member

"After my experience at this organization, I am no longer interested in working in fundraising." — Former fundraising professional

We heard each of these statements during the past week. These are not uncommon sentiments. However, they are not frequently voiced before people reach their breaking point.

With this column we share three proactive steps your organization can take to support board members and fundraising professionals.

Provide coaching and opportunities to learn. This is important for both board members and fundraising professionals. When board members are "told" they are responsible for making a personal gift and raising a specific amount of money they can be put off by what they perceive as a mandate. "I didn't sign up to fundraise," is the common complaint. Yet board members do have a fiduciary responsibility to the nonprofit organizations they govern. Take the time to learn the level of fundraising skill that each member possesses, and match these to your fundraising strategies. The same is true with staff. No one should be charged with "bringing in the money — no questions asked." That is not a winning strategy.

The board member we heard from last week said he made the required gift and then resigned. He didn't share his reasons for removing himself with the board president. The nonprofit lost a board member without gaining insight into how to prevent the situation from repeating itself.

Provide leadership. An executive director, president, or CEO needs to lead the organization and hold people accountable. That means she needs to know fundraising as well as the roles and responsibilities of board members and staff. The executive needs to ensure board members don't take charge of operations, directing staff on what to do. Likewise, she needs to hold staff accountable for reaching agreed-upon goals — note the phrase "agreed-upon." No one can mandate anything to anyone and expect smooth results. Fundraising professionals know their responsibilities and are often eager to expand these. At the same time, they know they are not miracle workers. They need the involvement of board members, the executive, and local stakeholders.

The fundraising professional we talked with last week was exasperated by how he was treated by the board. His work was not respected, the constraints he was operating under were not acknowledged, and he was publicly humiliated. *That is not a program for retaining professionals.*

Know your roles and responsibilities and fulfill them. Board members and fundraising professionals have distinct responsibilities. They need to work together, but each needs to understand his or her own role. Staff focuses on managing and implementing strategy and people; board members focus on policy, in addition to cultivating and soliciting major gifts. The fundraising plan should outline roles and responsibilities for staff and board.

Neither should be insulted by professional development opportunities such as coaching, workshops, strategy sessions, and role playing.

Our guidance: Work from a plan, stay in your lane, and don't take over other people's responsibilities.

First published November 7, 2016.

Advice for Board Members

Before You Say I Do

Responsibility

You've been asked to serve on the board of a nonprofit you believe in. It could be a college, a local advocacy organization, or a health care center. Do you say yes? What would you actually be saying yes to? What do you need to know to make an informed decision?

Board service is more than a resume-builder or image enhancer. It is work. That work includes responsibility for fundraising as well as oversight of the fundraising process. In order to make an informed decision, request a meeting with the board chair and the executive director. Requesting such a meeting communicates the seriousness you attach to board service. The answers you receive will let you know what is expected of you. They will also make visible the organization's fundraising strengths and challenges. Note: If the leadership doesn't have time to meet with you as a prospective board member, that may signal their inaccessibility and/or the lack of seriousness they attach to board membership.

Here are some questions you may want to ask. Add or subtract from the following list as appropriate. Use your list when meeting with the board chair and executive director.

Is the institution working from a strategic plan and a fundraising plan? What are the fundraising needs of the organization and what will it take to raise the required funds? What methods of fundraising are being used and how successful have these been? What percentage of funds is raised using what methods? What percentage of the budget comes from earned income, fees, or tuition? What are the opportunities and challenges the institution faces in the area of fundraising? Is there a reserve fund or endowment? What is the skill set of staff responsible for fundraising? What percentage of the CEO's time is spent on fundraising? What is the track record over the last five years?

What are the fundraising-related roles and responsibilities of board members as individuals and as a collective? Are there requirements for board members to give and fundraise? What percentage of annual funds is raised by the board? Are there orientation sessions to inform and equip board members for fundraising? What data management system is being used and what information is available to support board members and their fundraising? What is the average gift from the board?

What you learn by asking these questions can help you gauge how you can be of greatest support. At the end of the day, fundraising is absolutely critical to the survival of every nonprofit organization and institution. Don't be afraid to ask — the answers will help you provide the best leadership and oversight possible.

First published February 6, 2012.

Are You On Board?

Expectation

You've said "yes" and now are serving on the board. What is expected of you? How do you demonstrate leadership? While we don't have a crystal ball, we can provide guidance regarding your fundraising-related roles and responsibilities.

For many nonprofits, fundraising is often the major method for securing funds and resources. As a board member your leadership in this area makes a difference. Your roles and responsibilities fall into two general categories: policy and oversight, and giving and securing funds.

As a board member you will be asked to set fundraising policy. This includes tasks such as approving plans for special fundraising campaigns and setting gift acceptance policies. For example, when the university you serve decides to launch a $150 million fundraising campaign, that will come before the board for approval. You will want to ask informed questions such as, "What do the results of the feasibility study indicate?" Or, "How many lead donors have been identified?" In the area of gift acceptance policies, you may be asked to determine whether the organization will accept gifts of land, or cash gifts from gun manufacturers or tobacco companies.

You will also want to promote accountability and transparency. Support the adoption and implementation of policies related to conflicts of interest and whistleblower protection. Produce and distribute an annual report that shows how the organization uses the funds it receives. File your federal 990 on time. Communicate how the organization meets public needs and be willing to modify programs to help ensure the best use of resources.

On a day-to-day level, you will be responsible for understanding the institution's fund development plan and in helping bring it to life. For example, if the current focus is strengthening individual giving, you will want to participate in house or office parties your organization hosts so you can meet new potential donors and supporters and share with them the important work of the institution. As a board member your hospitality and words carry meaning and influence.

You should know the executive director's or president's vision for the institution. Talk with her. Ask questions. Then share that vision with other board members and with those who can provide funding and resources. Join your executive director when she meets with leaders of local foundations or corporations. Meet with her in advance to understand the purpose of each meeting and then participate, showing support for her leadership and answering questions as appropriate.

Most importantly, make your own gift. Make a meaningful gift every year. Ask the company you work for to make a gift or sponsor an event. You have to give and advocate. Set an example. Stretch a little. Your community needs you!

First published February. 10, 2012.

What Exactly Am I Supposed to Do?

A board member's fundraising responsibilities include knowing your nonprofit, knowing your role, and knowing your fellow board members, as well as making your own gift first before asking others to join you. Ready to begin? Here are some specific actions you can take to support your organization's fundraising:

1. **Make a personal gift.** Make it meaningful — more than a token gift. Your gift should be one of the largest you make each year, and should reflect your commitment to the organization.

2. **Raise three times the amount that you give.** Ask others to join you in giving at the same level, or greater.

3. **Don't go it alone.** Work with a fundraising partner. Create teams within your board, and then add a few non-board members to your team. You don't have to be a board member to raise funds for an organization. In fact, some people would prefer to be involved with fundraising and not serve on the board.

4. **Solicit major gifts.** In most cases it will take as much time and energy to solicit a $100 gift as it will to secure a $1,000 gift. Focus first on those who can give at the higher levels.

5. **Host an event at your home, office, or house of worship.** Make sure you have partner. Invite coworkers, friends, neighbors, and family. Share your organization's story and opportunities to get involved and give. Pay for the costs of the event; don't ask for reimbursement. Do this at least once each year.

6. **Participate in fundraising solicitations.** Accompany the executive director or development director on visits to potential donors. When appropriate, consider making the ask. Take the lead in following up.

7. **Give and help secure in-kind gifts and services.** These can include legal services, accounting, web design, social media, facilitation, printing, airline tickets, housing, and more.

8. **Cultivate potential donors.** Take the time to talk with people who have the combined interest and ability to give. Share the story of your organization. Invite them to an event. Introduce them to engagement opportunities.

9. **Collectively raise 10–20 percent of the annual budget.** As a board commit to raising a percentage of the organization's budget. Figure out your strategies and methods. Put these into action.

10. **Meet monthly to advance fundraising-related activities of the board.** These won't happen on their own. You need to plot, plan, report, respond, and adjust your strategies to meet your goal on time.

Don't wait to be asked to do something. Take the initiative and give without being asked (and don't give small!). Be proactive, but don't start any fundraising without coordinating your activities with the board and the executive director. They are a key part of your team.

First published July 23, 2018.

How to Be a Successful Board Member

Board service is critical to the success of a college or any nonprofit organization. Critical roles include fundraising and the hiring and evaluation of the president.

Dr. Belle Wheelan knows a lot about boards. As a former college president, she has worked with boards at two different institutions. She has served as a trustee, and currently works with a board in her role as president of the Southern Association of Colleges and Schools Commission on Colleges. Here, she shares her suggestions for how board members can position their president or CEO for success, reminding us that success for the president means success for the institution.

First, an ideal board will be made up of a diverse group of individuals, all bringing different areas of knowledge to the table. The board needs diverse collective knowledge and expertise in order to provide oversight and select a president. "You need board members who are more than friends of the college. They need expertise in banking and budgeting and long-range planning. Too often their skills are not the reason people are appointed. Too often these are self-perpetuating boards," she said.

Additionally, the board plays a vital role in supporting the institution's president, especially when there has been a change in leadership. "Boards need to be prepared to welcome a new president into the community. If the board chair lives out of town, the advancement person should be prepared to introduce the new president, but ideally it should be the entire board. The president should absolutely never have to introduce himself or herself to the community," she said.

As the president (or executive director) finishes his or her first year, it is important for the board to guard against potentially high or unrealistic expectations, and not grade him or her too harshly on her performance. Dr. Wheelan suggests several questions to use when evaluating performance:

- Did you stay in the budget you inherited?
- How informed did you keep the board on what is going on?
- How much money did you raise (if that is an expectation for the first year)?
- How many meetings did you have with people who could make a difference in the budget (if this is an expectation)?

She makes it clear that the board should identify a few things that are measurable and evaluate the president against these. Criteria that should not be used include, "She didn't give me football tickets," or, "I didn't like his wife's dress."

Dr. Wheelan also shared with us things the board should avoid. They should not tell the president how to run the institution. "It is tough when you know how you would do things, and you have to sit back and let the president lead. If you don't like the way the president is leading, then you get a new president. The board is not to lead," she said. "Your responsibilities are policy making and fiduciary oversight — not to go around the president to the staff. The president is the only person who works for you, the board. The staff works for the president."

We close with these words from the late Dr. Fred Lange, president of the Dallas Community Chest: "No institution can obtain greatness by stumbling over its board."

First published August 8, 2016.

You Can't Sell What You Don't Know

Passion

Mike Bruns possesses the characteristics of an ideal board member: deeply engaged with the organizations he supports, generous as a donor, and he treats his nonprofit involvement with the same seriousness he applies to business ventures. He has a great sense of humor, a kind heart, and a warm smile. He's also the founder of Comtrak Logistics, a national transportation and logistics company headquartered in Memphis, and chairman emeritus of Youth Villages, a national nonprofit. We recently talked with Bruns to learn the secrets to his success as a nonprofit volunteer leader.

We asked what he looks for in a nonprofit when deciding whether or not to become involved. His response was straightforward: "I do not want to be a part of an organization that is a fixer-upper, or is trying to make payroll by Friday. I want to support organizations who want to grow to the next level. The 'heart tug' is always trumped by an organization that is well run. With a well-run organization I can work with other board members to help grow it to the next level," he said.

It's not that he is opposed to the "heart tug." In fact, Bruns is passionate about the organizations he is involved with. "I truly believe in the organizations I become a part of. And I expect that of fellow board members. There's nothing worse than leadership that is begrudging or 'résumé building.' The secret to success lies in the passion of the leadership," he said.

Equally straightforward were his comments regarding expectations of fellow board members in the area of fundraising. He cited a lack of board giving as the number one obstacle to fundraising success. "There's nothing worse than a board member soliciting money and they haven't made a meaningful gift. It doesn't always have to be all money — it can be meaningful giving of time. But they have to believe in the organization and be engaged," he said.

Comparing fundraising to sales, Bruns was critical of board members who are not qualified to "sell the product." For that he places responsibility squarely on the shoulders of leadership: "What is the orientation? Without proper training, orientation, knowledge, feeling, and involvement, a board member can't 'sell' the nonprofit to potential donors. You can't sell what you don't know or believe in."

On the topic of giving, Bruns has learned personally that success in business is not enough, and that nonprofit involvement — and giving — can be even more exciting. "A person realizes that the 'buzz' you get from sharing can be greater than the buzz you get from daily life in business. Ten percent growth year after year doesn't always equal the buzz of giving 10 percent to the community," he said.

"The true donor misses the boat if they don't get just as much back in their heart, meeting people and making friends," Bruns continued. "Involvement brings satisfaction. It makes the donor feel good. I was chair of Youth Villages for so many years, and they did as much for me as I could ever do for the organization."

Youth Villages, also headquartered in Memphis, is a leading nonprofit dedicated to providing the most effective local solutions to help emotionally and behaviorally troubled children and their families live successfully.

"Youth Villages grew as a result of a wonderful culture, incredible leadership team, and a management team that knew this was a business. Nonprofit is more than a feel-good. Many stall out because the person who started the organization didn't surround themselves with good businesspeople. At Youth Villages the leadership surrounded themselves with businesspeople who helped them run the organization like a business, but not at the expense of their passion. They serve 60,000 young people and they measure everything. 'Feel good' doesn't last long if the business model doesn't work," he said.

That goes for the board as well. The biggest challenges Bruns has experienced arise when board members don't know what is expected of them. "That has to be done on the front end. You can't read a board manual to people. You need to explain their job description, financial expectations, and share with them why they were recruited. They have to become involved with the organization and passionate about it," he said. "Board members who are engaged and feel a part of something come to meetings. This solves the problem some boards have where they spend almost half their time worrying about the best time to get attendance. As board chair I focused on getting engagement. So many boards operate without engagement."

Bruns closed with his perspective on board members' reluctance to fundraise: "When a board member is not prepared and is not personally passionate, the gifts he solicits become a 'trap' wherein he now 'owes' an equal gift to the donor's nonprofit of choice." The solution? "Be prepared and sell the nonprofit on its merits, then people will give to the organization and not to you. You then are free to make your gifts based on merit."

First published August 5 and 12, 2013.

Key Duties of All Board Members

We recently had the opportunity to work with an organization that is ready to increase its impact. Current board members had recruited and approved new board members, and there was work to be done and people to do it. Our role was to help orient all members to their roles and responsibilities.

We structured the workshop around content included in *What Every Board Member Should Know: A Guidebook for Tennessee Nonprofits* published by the Tennessee Attorney General, Tennessee Secretary of State, and Center for Nonprofit Management. The guidebook is free and available online, is easy-to-understand, and applicable beyond Tennessee.

At the heart of all board responsibilities is "duty." These include the duties of good faith, loyalty, and care. These are defined as a board member's "fiduciary responsibilities." The big question is, what does fiduciary mean? It's not a term people use every day, but it is at the core of nonprofit governance. It is the legal and moral obligation to act in the best interest of another. At its core there is the expectation of trust. It is imperative for board members to place the interests of the nonprofit before their own, and to not seek personal benefit from board service.

Board members must know and understand the activities and financial condition of the organization. You cannot be fair to your nonprofit if you do not know what is going on. The following is a high-level summary of how individual board members fulfill their fiduciary duties:

- Attend board and committee meetings.
- Carefully read all material you receive, ask questions, and be active in board discussions.
- Use your own judgment in voting.
- Participate in strategic planning activities that assess and plan for the organization's future.
- Inquire whether there is a director's and officer's liability policy.
- Review board and committee minutes to ensure proper recording.
- Sign a conflict of interest statement at the start of each year.

It is also important that the board as a whole knows their responsibilities. This collective responsibility is fulfilled through engagement. Board members should:

- Hold regular board and committee meetings.
- Encourage open discussion.
- Pursue the mission and the organization's best interests with determination.
- Put a conflict of interest policy in place, and ensure it is reviewed annually.

- Take responsibility to ensure the nonprofit:
  - Operates in a fiscally sound manner.

- Has mechanisms in place to keep it fiscally sound.
- Is properly using any restricted funds it may have.

Here's the good news and the bad news: You have to show up for board meetings. Having your name on a board list is not enough. And showing up is not enough. You have to be engaged. At times this can mean asking difficult questions. Don't just "go along." You have a fiduciary responsibility to those your organization serves. We know you care — that's why you're on the board. The next step is to ensure you and your fellow board members exercise care.

First published April 3, 2017.

Six Simple Tasks to Energize Yourself and Your Board

Value

Do you sometimes wonder what value you bring to the nonprofits you serve as a board member? Do you wish you were more engaged, or that "they" took more advantage of the talents you bring to the board? We have the solution for you: Take initiative! Don't wait for someone to ask you to get involved.

Here are six things you can do between now and the next board meeting to energize yourself and your fellow board members. Choose one or more that sounds like fun to you. Each can help engage new supporters, increase awareness, and raise money. These tips work if you are involved with university, a grassroots organization, or any size nonprofit in between.

First, write a thank-you note or personally call a donor to thank them for their gift. Allocate five minutes for the conversation. Ask what encouraged them to give and what attracts them to your organization. Listen. Respond to any questions they may have. Thank them again.

Second, invite a potential supporter to visit the organization's facilities and observe its programs. Agree on a date and time to meet at the nonprofit and tour together. Request that a staff member join you — one who can share information and answer questions.

Third, visit staff members to get to know them and ask, "what can I do to help?" Follow through on what you learn.

Fourth, have lunch with a fellow board member to discuss how the two of you can work together to increase awareness or raise funds. Hatch a plan that can be implemented without staff involvement. Follow through on your ideas.

Fifth, make arrangements to speak before a local organization to share information about your nonprofit. It could be your church, the Rotary, or your book club. Keep your comments brief and engaging.

Sixth, host a small fundraising event. Invite a few close friends and associates to your home or office for coffee or an evening glass of wine. Spend five minutes sharing information about the nonprofit you serve and ask each guest to make a gift equal to or greater than your gift.

Before implementing these suggestions, take a moment to identify the three things you want to communicate about why you give your time and talent to serve on the board. Share these in conversation or through your presentation. Let people know you are accessible if they have questions in the future or if they want to get involved. Share your contact information. Bring a simple brochure to share.

Any one of these activities will extend the reach of your nonprofit. They will energize you. You will have something new to report at the next board meeting. Don't wait for someone to assign you to a task. Jump in!

First published March 24, 2014.

Board Responsibility for Financial Health

Wellbeing

The financial health of an organization is often attributed to the board of directors. The composition of the board, its actions, the level of giving, and the recognition of individual members all impact financial health.

Below you will find symptoms of board health and compromised health. Use these to evaluate the boards you are involved with. Join with your fellow board members to evaluate how healthy you are as a group. If you need to improve your health, you can.

Symptoms of fundraising health:

1. **Board members represent a diverse cross section of individuals with power, wealth, and influence.** The participation of people who can make a difference in the financial health of your organization is critical.

2. **The organization and its mission are a priority in the personal and professional lives of board members.** Those

who know you should know just how important board service is to you.

3. **Board members, volunteers, and staff work together from a fund development plan.** Coordinating all fundraising activities allows your institution to secure the maximum yield on its fundraising efforts.

4. **Board members make meaningful financial gifts.** As a board member it is your responsibility to make a "stretch" gift each year. Your donation should be one of the largest that you and your family will make during the year. An organization cannot expect others to give if the leadership is unwilling to do so.

5. **Board and staff evaluate their efforts and outcomes on an annual basis.** Evaluation helps all members determine what impact they are making and how they can best contribute to the organization's financial health.

6. **Board members and volunteers use their contacts to secure meaningful gifts and to open doors.** As a board member you can personally introduce new supporters to the institution and encourage their involvement.

7. **The organization is included in the estate plans of board members and volunteers.** As you plan for the financial future of your family members, consider also including a gift to benefit the organizations you serve.

8. **Board members are accessible and involved.** Don't just sit on a board — get involved. Give of your time, attend meetings, and engage others.

9. **Board members recruit new members who are equally or more influential.** It is up to you to ensure that future board members can provide the leadership and funding required for the fulfillment of your organization's mission.

Symptoms of compromised health:

1. **Community members and stakeholders cannot identify the organization's leadership.** When individuals, foundations, and granting agencies consider making a gift they often look at the board to see if it represents the constituency served, and if it includes local or national leadership, thought-leaders, and individuals of financial means. Some donors look at the board list first before reviewing other materials.

2. **All responsibility lies with staff.** When staff is responsible for fundraising, you can rest assured that you are not raising the money you could. People give to people and to those who are volunteering their time and donating their own money. When staff takes on the responsibility of fundraising, it is often because board members are not fully enough engaged to ask others to give.

3. **Finger-pointing without offering solid solutions.** No one likes to be criticized. But most of us are eager to improve. Suggestions that address current challenges are welcomed, especially when you are willing to help create the change you want to see.

4. **Lack of individual leadership and initiative.** For a board to be collectively strong, individual members need to demonstrate leadership and initiative by taking on projects that impact the institution's finances or programs.

5. **Sparse attendance at key meetings.** When attendance starts to dwindle, it is time to look at meeting content. Are members asked to passively sit through staff reports? Are they engaged in projects they report on? Are you simply "meeting to meet"?

6. **Inactivity renders board members and volunteers a liability.** Without assigned tasks board members can focus on areas that are not a priority, creating more work and taking an organization off track.

7. **All talk and no action.** There's only so much free advice an organization can use. Board members need to help put their suggestions into action.

8. **Members are satisfied with the status quo.** The board should be future-focused and looking for ways to improve advocacy, education, and/or services. Members should be cultivating future leadership, evaluating the organization's direction, and updating its strategic plan.

9. **Members are unable to make the case for financial support.** The key to making the case is knowing the organization's top three fundraising priorities and their potential impact.

As with physical health it is best to know if you have a "health challenge." Untreated challenges can lead to unwanted consequences. Too often the biggest challenge lies in not knowing you have a challenge. The first step is diagnosis.

First published December. 26, 2016 and January. 2, 2017.

Fundraising Tips for Board Members

Summer is often the season for nonprofit board retreats. We have been asked to facilitate a few recently, with a focus on the role of the board in fundraising. Our clients want to know tips, best practices, and specific ways that board members can increase their involvement.

With this column we share with you three suggestions you can use as a board member — and you collectively can use as a board.

Know your nonprofit.

Before you become involved with fundraising, take time to learn the nuts and bolts of the organization you serve. We know you are committed, but how much do you know about programs, advocacy, impact, staffing, revenue, and partnerships? Can you quantify the organization's impact? Do you know the environment the nonprofit is working in? Most importantly, do you know the executive director's vision for the organization? Do you believe in it? Are your actions as an individual board member in sync with her vision? Is the board as a collective body organized to advance her vision? Do you know the executive director?

Related to this, do you know what the organization is raising money for? Do you know the current fundraising goal and how funds raised will be used? For example, is the organization expanding specific programs, implementing technology to reach additional families, or funding scholarships to increase the number of women in engineering?

Know your role and know your fellow board members.
You need to know why you were recruited to the board and the role that your fellow board members and the executive director expect you to fulfill. Are these in sync with your understanding? Have you received written information about your role and responsibilities as a board member? If yes, have you read it recently? If not, ask for this. Take time to contemplate and document why you are serving on the board. What skills, experience, resources, and relationships do you bring? How and when are you willing to share these? Write this down. Make a commitment to yourself and share it with your fellow board members.

Take the time to personally get to know your fellow board members. Who are they as individuals, family members, professionals, artists, or political leaders? What are their interests and experiences? Where do they live and work? What is their expertise and skills? What do they think about the work of your nonprofit? How do they want to be involved? What are their aspirations? How can you work together? If your board doesn't already have a "buddy system," consider implementing one. The buddy system is simply a process of teaming board members to work together toward a fundraising goal. Members get to know each other, work together, and to set and reach a fundraising goal. A benefit of the buddy system is increased accountability between and fellowship amongst board members.

Make your own gift first, then ask others to join you.
Once you know why you are giving it is easier to ask others to join you. Talk with people you know and let them know why you are involved with your nonprofit. Share why you give and ask others to make a similar gift. Using the buddy system, work with a fellow board member to host a home or office event to introduce your

nonprofit. Ask your friends and family to give in honor of your birthday. Set a goal for how much you want to raise and spend time each month cultivating and soliciting gifts.

First published July 18, 2018.

Combat Planned Confusion During Board Meetings

Does your board or committee meet over and over without gaining any traction, let alone achieving anything that could be considered success or just completion? If you answer yes, you may be suffering from planned confusion.

Sometimes we are our own worst enemy. And, what's worse, we don't know it. Or even worse, we know exactly what we are doing — we set things up so it's hard to point fingers and difficult to remedy the situation. As the name implies, planned confusion is planned. Sometimes consciously, sometimes unconsciously. It has symptoms and causes. Here are a few — are any of these familiar?

Symptoms. We try to schedule meetings, but they keep getting postponed at the last minute. The person who is supposed to take notes or minutes doesn't distribute them, and when he does, they don't include action items or agreed-upon next steps. When we meet, we have to start from the beginning because many people were unable to attend the last meeting and need to be brought up to speed.

And, we don't have an agenda, or we have one that lacks specificity. As a board, we lack a quorum, so when we meet we are not conducting official business. At meetings we constantly hear from people with no track record or integrity — they don't do what they say they will do. We get frustrated by our inability to neutralize "meeting bullies" — those who talk loudly, flex their muscles, and intimidate others from participating.

More symptoms. We have a culture of excuses and the result is that people don't do what they say they will do. When we make decisions, the follow-up activities are not completed on time. We suspect that our fellow members really don't care — they are participating because they have to. We lack the courage to look at the underlying issues that need to be addressed. We present issues, ideas, and thoughts that go against our stated goals and objectives, or proposed/identified solutions. We don't have defined goals, objectives, and expectations. We don't know what we are trying to achieve, and we don't have a timeline. When we do move forward, people are unable to "stay in their lane" — they focus on the work and responsibilities of others instead of their own project. We don't need anyone from the outside to undercut our momentum — we do it ourselves.

Causes. Underneath these symptoms there are usually a few causes. These include a lack of defined purpose or an outdated vision, the wrong people on the board, a lack of leadership, poor communication, and/or lack of consistent follow-up between meetings. Being honest is the first step in finding out what's really going on. If you are committed, then you need to speak up. Talk to your board members offline. Learn their perspectives. Be sure to keep your word, and then begin the process of holding people accountable to their word.

First published June 5, 2017.

Got a Minute for the Minutes?

We recently facilitated two board meetings for two very different types of organizations. One was an institution that is over 100 years old with a multimillion-dollar budget. The other was an emerging grassroots, community-based organization. At both meetings the focus was fundraising, and board members were actively engaged.

Members had suggestions about how to make or improve the case for support, who to engage as leadership-level volunteers, how to develop, explore, or advance meaningful partnerships, and how to strengthen the board. Decisions were made regarding committees, timeframes, and next steps. Another similarity between the two groups: Both agreed that board giving is a must, and that board members should take the lead in raising funds.

We felt energized leaving both meetings. We were optimistic about actions that board members would take, and the potential for each board to move their respective organization forward. Yet when we reviewed the minutes for each meeting we were left uninspired.

What? Minutes should be inspiring? Well, we think so. When they are simply a record of what was said, you have to read through the contents in their entirety, and highlight the action items in order to create an easy-to-use record of next steps that includes who agreed to do what by when.

Our suggestion: Record minutes in a way that works with the history, culture, and requirements of your organization or institution. Supplement these with a list of next steps and agreements that clearly communicates decisions made and work to be accomplished, including who is responsible for each task and the timeframe. Email these to all participants within 48 hours. If you have the capacity, you may want to personalize each message so it lists the member's individual commitments and related timeframes directly in the body of the email for easy access.

We believe that board members have a critical role in fundraising that extends beyond the board meeting. When members quickly receive a message focused on next steps they can get into action and draw on the momentum created during the board meeting.

Here are three other ways that user-friendly minutes help advance fundraising.

1. Minutes neutralize subjectivity. People may recall things differently, and memories can slip, especially if the board is meeting monthly or quarterly.

2. Minutes give your organization legitimacy. They reinforce accountability and transparency by documenting agreements. They make visible any tasks that remain undone and they mitigate against fundraising stall.

3. Minutes help you stay focused, making sure you have consistent progress in spite of things that come up between meetings. They create a sense of urgency. Those who attended can quickly see what they are responsible for and begin taking action so tasks can be completed on time.

Distributing timely minutes is a momentum builder. It says the meeting was important and you must keep moving forward. It also indicates how well the organization is being managed.

First published May 16, 2016.

Board Summer Refreshers

Involvement

Contemplate these "board refreshers" as you enjoy your summer. Grab your board binder, put on your nonprofit sun visor, and let's talk board engagement.

Let's start by pulling out the bylaws for the nonprofit you serve. If you can't find your copy, or never received one, request a copy from the board chair or executive director. Read them. Mark them up. What do you understand? What doesn't make sense? Do they appear to be up-to-date or out-of-date? Here are a few basic things you want to know. Are there term limits for members? What is the maximum size of the board? What constitutes a quorum? Reach out to the board chair with your questions. Ask for answers. Chances are that if you have questions, so do others.

Next up for review is the budget. Study it closely. What information is clear and what raises questions? How does the current fiscal year compare to the prior year? Is the budget increasing without an increase in fundraising or grant revenue? Have there been transfers from endowment to the operating budget? Were the prior year's revenue goals met? If your organization is audited, review the audit. Do you know what is being communicated and what you should look out for when providing oversight? Look closely at the fundraising goals and what was actually raised. And look at your own checkbook. Did you make a gift? Did you participate in fundraising with fellow board members?

Think about the board meetings themselves. What happened during the meetings you attended? How many did you make? If attendance was a challenge for you, look at the reason why. Was the issue scheduling, or could it be you're just not that interested? If scheduling is at the heart of the matter, speak with your board chair to get the issue resolved. If your interest or commitment has waned, that's fine. Again, speak with your chair and coordinate the how and when of resigning. There is no stigma to leaving a board if your heart isn't in it. Effective boards — and by extension effective nonprofits — need committed and engaged members.

When reflecting on the past year's board meetings, think about what was accomplished by the board and how the time in board meetings was actually spent. What were your feelings at meetings? Were you bored, engaged, energized, confused? Take a moment to write up your suggestions for how to increase the level of board engagement. Share these with the board chair at the appropriate time.

Finally, look to the future. What do you want to accomplish as a board member in the coming year? Is there one thing that you want to take responsibility for? How will you work with your fellow board members to accomplish your goal?

First published July 24, 2017.

Supporting Interim Leadership

One of the biggest changes within the life of a nonprofit is a change in leadership. In most cases this will be accompanied by a period of transition with an interim leader. The position is short-term, and in most cases, temporary. We have seen interims who serve as placeholders or caretakers. Others are innovators. Some are turn-around leaders. Others are brought in explicitly to "clean house."

The experience can be tumultuous, or a breath of fresh air. What actually happens within an organization during this time is highly contingent upon the actions of the board, the culture of the organization, and the person who serves as the interim leader. Finally, the terms under which the prior leader left will also impact how the organization transitions into the future. In all cases it will be a change.

Questions for board members.
What are you looking for the interim leader to accomplish? Will you ask her to retain talented employees and stop the trend of employee resignations that can accompany the departure of a president or CEO? Do you need her to reduce the number of employees or

change the employee composition to better respond to market needs? Do you expect the interim to sustain the current level of fundraising? Increase fundraising? Do you need to decrease costs, increase services, implement new technology, sustain current operations, or build new partnerships? The expectations need to be clearly established and communicated.

As a board you may need to be more actively involved in matters related to strategic directions, fundraising, policy, and finances. Are you prepared, individually and collectively, to support the interim leader you hire?

Questions for interim leaders.
If you are asked to serve as an interim you may already be affiliated with the organization or institution as a board member or employee. You may have prior experience as an executive, or you may possess a specific skill set that the nonprofit needs at this point in time. It's also possible that you are an experienced interim leader. In all cases you need to ask questions and gather information before you accept or decline. You will want to learn the challenges facing the organization, its history, and its vision for the future.

Key things to ask about are the strategic plan and the extent to which it is being implemented. What is the community's perception of and relationship to the organization? Is the nonprofit looking to grow, consolidate, transform, or innovate? What is the projected duration of the position? You'll need to ask about the organization's current and projected finances and who will lead fundraising. You'll want to know who you can depend upon to introduce you throughout the community, and you need to know who your friends and advocates will be and who may be working against you.

Whether you are hiring an interim leader or serving as one, having clear expectations can help reduce the stress that accompanies change. Keep the lines of communication open and know that this is a transition, not necessarily a new normal.

First published July 10, 2017.

Replace Yourself, Sustain Your Board

Replacement

It is neither good nor advisable to serve on a board forever. While you may be deeply committed to the organization or institution you serve, you need to rotate off the board at the appropriate time, at least for a little while. Term limits help a board sustain a freshness and new perspective that can be lacking when too many board members have served more than four or five years. It can be hard for an organization to change when its leadership is static and lacking in new ideas.

Rotating off the board can be good for the organization and good for you. Take a breather. Spend more time with your family. Take a class. Join the gym. Or volunteer for another board and learn how another organization approaches similar or different issues.

But, before you leave, you need to replace yourself. We know — you're irreplaceable. Given that truth, come as close as you can. Or, find someone to serve who could be an even more committed and engaged board member than you have been.

As a board member you know the organization's strengths and challenges, and the skill sets, relationships, and access to funding represented within the board. You can help identify someone with a different skill set, perspective, or constituency that will add value to the board.

Think about who you know, personally or professionally, who is committed to the values and mission of the organization. Take the time to introduce them to other board members in a social setting. Invite them to meet the CEO or executive director, and to witness the organization in action. Share with your friend or colleague why you serve on the board, and ask him or her to consider serving as well.

As a committed board member you are almost morally committed to ensure the organization can move forward with strong board leadership. Do not leave it to the CEO or board chair to replace you. Be proactive and identify potential new board members who can help take the organization to the next level of its growth. Express your commitment by identifying new leadership. While ultimately it is the responsibility of the development committee to recommend new board members to the full board for consideration, you can ensure a strong pool of potential candidates. You've been effective — now bring someone else in to help build on your success.

First published October 10, 2011.

What Will Be Your Fundraising Legacy?

Whether you are a new or established board member, we suggest you take the time to define for yourself what you want to accomplish through your service. Time will pass. Crises will arise. There will be leadership changes, budget shortfalls, unexpected windfalls, mergers, resignations, and more. You and your fellow board members will have to respond and react. In order to assure you are more than responsive, we suggest you set a fundraising-related goal that you consistently advance so when your board term ends, you will leave a legacy.

You set the goal. There are many to choose from. You could raise a specific amount of money, build a partnership with a business or corporation, develop and grow a revenue-generating special event, or grow an earned income stream. You might commit to serving as chair of the development committee of the board with the goal of creating a proactive fundraising culture within the board. You may choose to have your business, faith community, or sorority "adopt" the organization, giving time, money, and resources in a concentrated fashion. Depending on your experience, you might take the lead in evaluating the current management of your institution's endowment or your organization's reserve fund with the goal of reducing risk and fees.

Of course your goals need to benefit the organization you are serving. That is a must. Keep your eyes and ears open for those areas where your expertise, connections, and resources can make a difference. In most cases you should be able to quickly assess these. Talk with your fellow board members and appropriate staff to gain the input and guidance you need.

Seek to make a lasting change or impact. Put in place something that will continue to make a difference in the life of the institution or organization. It could be an event, a program, a policy, a procedure, a fundraising event, or an awareness event. Whatever it is, you want it to sustain beyond your board term.

For example, consider approaching your employer about creating a partnership with the community organization or college where you sit on the board. Analyze the needs of both and work to build a mutually beneficial long-term partnership. Or work with the executive director and CFO to create an annual line item for fundraising-related professional development, and then work to secure those funds. Or consider seeding an endowment with your giving and fundraising.

While your goals should dovetail and support those of the full board and executive management, do not wait to learn what others want you to do. Once you have an understanding of the organizational culture, priorities, assets, and challenges, make your move. Be assertive — make your goals known, or simply go to work knowing that the fruits of your labor will speak volumes.

Step into the leadership opportunity that is awarded to you as a member of the board. You can leave a legacy.

First published April 22, 2018.

Advice for All Nonprofit Leaders

Is Your Nonprofit Legit? Guidelines for Boards and Executives

Passion for mission is at the heart of a nonprofit, but don't forget your "business" requirements. Nonprofits must comply with many of the same regulations as businesses, plus additional ones that are specific to the sector. As an executive or board member you need to be aware of these and to operate within the law.

Paperwork

Make sure your "paperwork" is in order and shared with your board. All members should have a copy of the organization's IRS 501(c)(3) determination letter, mission statement, bylaws, and most recent tax filing. Each year the 990 IRS form needs to be submitted on time. If revenue is less than $50,000, you can file the simple 990N — it is a postcard with eight questions. Depending on state law, you may be required to file with the state prior to launching a fundraising campaign. Fundraising counsel or contractors may also need to register with the state.

Board agendas and minutes

All parties are best served when agendas are distributed well in advance of each board meeting. Board members are required to make informed decisions, and depend on advance receipt of information so each has time to review and contemplate items prior to discussion or a vote. Similarly, minutes should be distributed within 48 hours. While this is not a legal requirement, we suggest this policy as it supports timely and open communication and allows board members ample time between meetings to complete actions they committed to, and to research topics that may be continued at the next meeting.

Committees and policies

Your organization needs written policies and procedures that protect against error, fraud, and embezzlement. Policies should also protect whistleblowers — people who bring issues to the attention of the board or management, and who could be at risk of retribution. A conflict of interest policy should be in place and reviewed annually.

Board members must act in the best interests of the nonprofit. At its most basic level, this means you shouldn't look to profit from the organizations you serve. Any transactions with board members must always benefit the nonprofit. An example of this could be providing quality office space at below-market rates. In terms of committees, make sure you have an audit and finance committee that closely reviews financial information and ensures funds are properly invested and correctly accounted for. This includes ensuring that gifts and grants are used per donors' requirements.

Most states and major cities have an agency designed to assist and protect nonprofits and the people (constituents and donors) that support them. Staff and board members should be aware of and comply with these guidelines and regulations. You can check with your attorney general to learn more or you can visit the National Association of State Charity Officials website (www.nasconet.org) for resources specific to your state.

Not paying attention to guidelines and regulations can be a silent killer that disrupts your nonprofit without notice. Take time to know your responsibilities.

First published July 5, 2016.

Open, Honest Communication

Communication

Engaged and effective nonprofit board members are the dream of board chairs and executive directors. "If only our board members were more engaged" is a common refrain. "I can't keep fighting my board" is another. Board members also have concerns: "I don't know why we have board meetings — the executive makes the decisions and expects us to rubber-stamp them."

One perspective reflects a desire for board members to attend meetings regularly, to come prepared, to work with other board members between meetings, and to provide guidance and oversight that reflects a deep understanding of the organization's work. The second reflects a frustration, usually on the part of an executive director, that board members are not in alignment with the executive's vision and strategies. The third speaks to board members' confusion and disengagement.

There is one tactic that can assist with these three challenges: open, honest, in-person communication. Scheduling and thoughtfully preparing for conversations prior to a board meeting can change what happens at the meeting. It sounds simple, but it takes time, requires preparation, and needs to be applied consistently. The following are suggestions for how to employ this tactic.

If you are a board chair, make sure you know the vision of your executive director. What is she seeking to accomplish? How does she want to accomplish it? What will be the impact? What will it cost? What does she need from the board to bring her vision to life? Take time to learn her leadership and communication styles. Meet with her regularly and strategize how to best engage the full board and committees in advancing her vision. Work with her to create the board agenda, ensuring the concerns of both board members and the executive director are included.

If you are an executive director, take the time to meet regularly with your board chair, to share your strategic thinking, to ask for counsel, and to provide updates on operations. Form a partnership that acknowledges and respects your board chair's leadership, vision, expertise, and position. Asking for guidance and creating a shared agenda can help surface best thinking and create a strong partnership.

Both the executive director and the board chair should take time to meet individually with board members prior to each board meeting. This is especially important if the board meets quarterly, or less often. Each of you need to personally share updates and gain insights and involvement from individual board members. Take the time to share organizational updates and challenges, successes, strategies, and potential challenges. Listen to each board member's concerns, interests, and ideas. Act on those that you can.

It takes time to have these meetings. It also yields results. A nonprofit's board is one of its most valuable resources. Take the time to strengthen your relationships.

First published January 20, 2014.

Is Your Board Bored?

Boredom

Here's a question for our readers who are nonprofit executives and board members: Is your board fully engaged? Does the structure of your board meetings encourage members to bring their talents and abilities to the table or does it stifle members' creativity and create a "bored board"?

If you are a nonprofit executive, do you really know who is serving on your board? Do you know their skills, strengths, talents, and relationships? Do you have a strategy for how to engage each board member in advancing the agreed-upon goals of the organization? Have you met with each to share the current strategic plan and ask how each would like to be involved in bringing it to life?

Do you provide board members with information they need to serve as advocates and fundraisers? Have you met personally with members who tend to miss meetings, come unprepared, or are otherwise disengaged? Have you reflected on what you know about their skills, personality, and relationships and considered strategies for involving members in ways that are in line with their interests?

Do you typically create and circulate the board agenda? Do board members agree with the majority of your ideas? Do you have challenges getting a quorum at meetings? If you answered "yes," you may want to look at doing things differently.

Encourage your board chair to work collaboratively with you in crafting the agenda. Ask her to pose questions to the board — ask for their insights to challenges and opportunities the organization is grappling with. Find a way to creatively release the talents of your board. A "yes" board is not an asset. Not one of us is so wonderful that all our ideas are perfect. Encourage dialog and diversity of opinion.

If you are serving on a board, take a moment to reflect on your involvement. Why are you on the board? Is the reason you joined the board the reason you continue to serve? Are you serving at the request of your employer? Are you filling a seat that is reserved for a representative from your business, agency, church, or organization? Is your board service an obligation or a challenging joy? Do you attend the majority of board meeting? Do you participate or are you bored? Can you summon the courage to talk with the board chair and find a way to contribute to a positive change in how the board operates?

Here's what we know: Talented, respected, and well-connected people are often asked to serve on nonprofit boards. But, the structure of board meetings can work against their active involvement. A board's talent is lost when meetings are filled with reading of reports and discussions regarding the next time to meet. Consider working with a consent agenda and time allocated to strategic discussions regarding operations, growth, partnerships, and delivery of services. No need to be bored.

First published January 7, 2013.

The Power of Nonprofit Volunteer Leadership

Thriving

Volunteers play a key role in the life of nonprofits. They serve as board members, provide services and advocacy, and they donate their professional services. In the area of fundraising, the important role of volunteers cannot be overstated. Fundraising volunteers provide leadership and strategy. They open doors that can lead to meaningful funding or resources. They give gifts of their own and they cultivate and solicit others to do the same.

This is the model that is at the heart of thriving and successful nonprofits.

At the same time there are many nonprofits with volunteers who don't "step up" at the expected level. There are many reasons for this, all of which can result in less than optimal funding — and relationships — for nonprofits.

In this column we identify characteristics of volunteers who, in general terms, are not performing up to expectations.

Whether you are a board member, staff member, or volunteer at a nonprofit, you may have noticed some of the following "challenges" playing out within your organization.

- Fundraising leaders ask to serve "in name only" and are not joined at the hip with the CEO and fundraising staff.

- They fail to make a leadership-level gift to the campaign and do not provide motivation and encouragement to fellow fundraising leaders and volunteers.

- When you talk with these leaders, you notice they lack passion and enthusiasm.

- Or, conversely, they are very enthusiastic when speaking, but fail to follow through on their commitments.

- Some are unable to clearly make the case for the organization and the campaign, even though they are asked to do so in public.

- They may lack vision or be unable to provide resources that can advance an organization's fundraising.

Bottom line: They don't live up to expectations.

If the fundraising leadership within your organization displays more than a few of these characteristics, don't be alarmed. These issues are found in large established institutions as well as grassroots organizations. And, they can be addressed. The first step in the process is awareness of the problem. Without awareness, conflict can emerge between fundraising leaders, the board, executive director, and development staff. Finger-pointing begins with each party blaming the other. Each states that they want the organization to be successful, that they want to be involved with fundraising, but they can't do what they know they should do because other parties aren't fulfilling their responsibilities. This is the beginning of the blame game, which can go on for months and years. But it doesn't have to!

Understanding what is going on — and why — can help your organization move toward new results. It will take work, but it also takes work to focus on a goal you know won't be fulfilled.

First published January 7, 2018.

Building Consensus and Reaching Agreement

Agreement is the cornerstone upon which a healthy nonprofit is built. Without agreement amongst an organization's leadership, it is almost impossible to sustain successful fundraising.

You may be in a situation where there was agreement in the past, but changes in board membership, executive leadership, the economy, or the needs of the community have eroded the prior agreement. That's not necessarily a bad thing — it may be time for things to change.

Reaching and sustaining agreement is an ongoing process that impacts many aspects of your organization, including fundraising. For example, your case for support, fundraising priorities, and strategies all depend on prior agreement. Without agreement, leadership may feel they are asked to rubber-stamp decisions. They may consent in words but not with actions. You may find "simple" decisions such as approving a grant submission evolve into lengthy discussions that question the organization's direction. These can emerge because time was not previously allocated to full and open discussion.

Here's a process we suggest. Both the board chair and the executive director should schedule individual conversations with board members, senior staff, and key volunteers. The purpose of these conversations is to learn their thoughts regarding current and proposed programming, strategic directions, fundraising, staffing, and — in general terms — their level of comfort with the nonprofit and how they want to be involved. Questions should be answered, dissent noted and addressed, and new ideas given proper consideration.

These individual conversations should be followed by a leadership meeting. The board chair and executive director should communicate the work that lies ahead for the coming year and invite discussion. They can begin by laying out new ideas raised in individual conversations, or areas where they know there is dissent.

This may sound like "a lot of unnecessary work." Others may feel it "opens up a can of worms." We believe it is important to the very foundation of your nonprofit. Some years leaders may engage in long, animated discussions. Other years leadership may nod in agreement, reaffirming prior commitments and wanting to get on with the work at hand.

What's most important is that every attempt is made to understand minority opinions and objections. When people feel their concerns are not addressed, they can make it difficult to reach future decisions, or they may remove themselves from the organization, taking with them their wisdom and relationships.

Learn more by reading chapter one of our book *Prerequisites for Fundraising Success*.

First published January 5, 2016.

Should Board Members Give?

Donation

"My board doesn't give." That's a common lament we hear from executive directors and college presidents. Here's one from board members: *"They only want me for my money."*

Both statements may be true. If these sentiments are active within your organization or institution you might want to take a moment to think about what's underneath these.

If you are an executive director or president, consider the following.

How would you characterize your relationship with the board, and especially your board president? Do you feel responsible for the board's actions? Do you feel like you have to do the board's work because they just won't step up? Do you wish the board would just do what they should do? Do you feel you have to spend too much time with your board? What are your expectations and what are they based on? Are they realistic? Have you shared them with your board chair and the chair of your development or fundraising committee? What are the processes you use for setting the organization's fundraising goals, and how do you involve the board? Do you know the individuals who sit on the board of your organization? Do you wish the board would just raise money so you could do more important things?

If you are a board member, consider the following.

What is your assessment of the organization in general? Do you feel comfortable asking questions in board meetings, or personally in conversation with the board chair or executive director? Do you have a good understanding of the organization's goals, successes, and limitations? Do you hold the organization to standards they may not be able to meet? Deep in your heart, do you find you are "sitting on the board" instead of "serving on the board"? What would need to change in order for you to make a meaningful gift and ask others to do so? Do you feel that people see you for your money and don't see the other ways in which you can contribute? Do you feel that you don't have the capacity to give in the way other board members do? What impact do you want to make on the organization you serve?

Here's what we have learned from our experience.

Sometimes it is easier to silently point the finger at others or to dream of a perfect organization than it is to honestly assess what's going and what can be done to create a culture change. Sometimes the reason board members aren't engaged in fundraising are structural. This refers to issues such as whether the organization is working from a plan, whether there are defined roles and responsibilities, the experience and giving capacity of board members, the use of technology, the format of board meetings, and the skill set of the board chair, executive director, and development staff.

Take the time to assess what's really going on. Assess your capacity and begin building infrastructure. Your board can become a giving board.

First published January 29, 2018.

How to Increase Board Giving and Fundraising

Should board members give? Our answer is yes. And, they should fundraise. That doesn't mean you don't need fundraising professionals. You do. But don't think for a minute that they can be successful without a partnership with an engaged board. Here we share a few specific things you can do to increase board giving and fundraising.

For executive directors, presidents, and development directors:

1. Be honest. Tell the truth, and don't paint a rosy picture that somehow overlooks current or anticipated challenges.

2. Ask for guidance and input from your board.

3. When meeting with potential new board members, communicate giving and fundraising expectations. Share a copy of board member roles and responsibilities as they relate to fundraising and development.

4. Clearly communicate the organization's priorities and how fundraising goals tie to these. Be clear on what you are raising money for and why.

5. Share the following:

   - Past fundraising results, plans, opportunities, and challenges

   - The type of support available to board members from staff and each other

   - Past results of board giving and initiatives

   - The types of data and reports that will be shared with them throughout the process

   - Sample pledge forms and commitment forms

6. Provide fundraising orientation and coaching sessions.

7. Meet with each board member to talk about their fundraising history and things they would like to do, as well as things they are not comfortable with. Ask about the resources and skill sets each has — or may have access to through their friends, family, and associates.

8. Talk about accountability.

9. Pair each new board member with another board member who is seasoned, experienced, and successful at fundraising

For board members:

1. Propose an awareness or fundraising event that you would take the lead on. Invite others to join you.

2. Recruit individuals with fundraising experience to join with you to implement your fundraising projects

3. Poll your fellow board members to learn their skill sets and what they are comfortable with as it relates to fundraising.

4. Don't expect everyone on the board to actively engage in fundraising. Define supportive roles for members to play that will impact fundraising.

5. Seek out resources and in-kind services that will support your fundraising efforts.

6. Discuss the types of support and tools needed for members to be successful.

7. Explore ways to make fundraising fun and meaningful. Encourage socializing after and between meetings.

8. Celebrate accomplishments! Acknowledge and reward short-term successes and milestones.

9. Stay focused on long-term projects, and what it will take to be successful.

Here's what we know: Everyone has to work together to ensure the financial health, vitality, and sustainability of an organization.

First published February 5, 2018.

Planning a Board Retreat

Rejuvenate

Summer is often associated with beaches, family vacations, hot sun, and good fun. For those in the nonprofit sector, summer is also the season for retreats. These are times set aside to focus on programming, strategy, growth, partnerships and, importantly, fundraising. While we believe in keeping the "fun" in fundraising, these retreats need to blend fun and business. Here we share a few suggestions for how to help ensure retreats are well planned for by both staff and board members.

Planning

If you are charged with helping to plan a retreat, we suggest you provide all participants with information well in advance. While not everyone will read and absorb the material, some people need time to contemplate what is being asked of them in order to best participate. There are others who don't appreciate surprises. If they are giving their time to a retreat, they want to know what is being asked of them. Sending materials in advance to all members helps to ensure full participation.

Create an agenda that includes opportunities for participants to interact and provide input. When the focus is fundraising make sure you clearly communicate fundraising goals and priorities, including how much needs to be raised for each priority. Share the tools available to support fundraising, and provide guidance on how to use these. Update participants on the processes to measure and evaluate progress toward goals. Include time for small group activities such as creating a timeline and activity chart to guide the work of staff and board members.

Participating

When you are a retreat participant you want to **stay aware of what is being asked of you before, during and after the retreat.** The following are a few items to track:

1. Do you understand the goals and mission set forth by the CEO?

2. Are you clear on ways in which you can become engaged?

3. Do you know what is asked of you and by when?

4. Is there commitment and buy-in from your fellow board members?

5. What support you can expect to receive from board members and staff?

Don't be afraid to ask questions. These can include:

1. What are the challenges we face? How can we overcome these?

2. What are we selling in the philanthropic marketplace for the upcoming year?

3. What has been the track record and success of the organization to date?

4. How will we be informed throughout the process?

5. Is there a written plan that has had input from board members, staff, and key stakeholders?

6. What is the plan B and plan C if plan A falters?

Retreats (or "advances" as some now refer to these gatherings) can be extremely productive — with advanced planning and full engagement by all participants. Prepare, participate, and then get to work!

First published July 17, 2017.

Assessing Last Year's Performance

Reflection

At the year's end, many of us reflect on the past and make promises for the future. We have visions of the wonderful things we will do personally, professionally, and most of all for the nonprofits we serve.

We have put together an exercise you can use individually, and then share with your fellow board members, staff, or volunteer team for a collective reflection. Review the following lists and evaluate, with a simple yes or no, what you were able to accomplish.

Board members. Were you able to:

1. Give or get a meaningful gift?

2. Propose a game-changing idea?

3. Secure an in-kind gift or service that enabled the organization to sustain and grow?

4. Recruit a board member with the specific skills your board is seeking?

5. Host an awareness event at your home or office?

6. Include your nonprofit as a part of your estate planning?

7. Observe another nonprofits in order to gain inputs, ideas, and strategies to enhance your service?

8. Meet personally with the CEO to see where you could be of help?

9. Share about your nonprofit via social media?

CEO/executive director. Did you:

1. Develop, or work from, a business plan to help sustain and grow your organization?

2. Work with staff to make necessary adjustments related to their job descriptions?

3. Personally meet with all members of the board to share your vision and goals?

4. Solicit the top 20 percent of your donors who generate 80 percent (or more!) of your funds?

5. Implement a plan to create awareness and involvement?

Chief fundraising officer or development director. Were you able to:

1. Put in place, or work with, a data management system that supports you in making critical fund development management decisions?

2. Recruit and train the volunteers you need to run your annual campaign?

3. Create and work from a timeline and activity chart that represents 18 months of work?

4. Meet with your CEO or executive director to learn what is expected of you, and what percentage of the annual fundraising goal you are expected to raise?

Volunteer leaders. Did you:

1. Make a meaningful gift to the organization?

2. Ask for and sign off on your documented roles and responsibilities?

3. Attend all key meetings and special events?

4. Review and provide input into the organization's case for support?

5. Participate in the recruitment of other volunteers and leaders?

6. Make the case to other individuals and organizations who could provide support?

First published December 30, 2018.

Recommit to Fundraising

Is fundraising at the top of your to-do list for next year? Are you ready to recommit to help ensure the vitality of your nonprofit or college? Will you sign your fundraising commitment form again? What?!? Your organization doesn't use one? Now is the time to change that. Here are three suggestions for how you can make a difference in your organization's fundraising.

If you are a fundraising or development professional: Review the commitment forms that board members completed last year. Set up a time to meet with each member to review and plan for the coming year. Meeting in person is ideal, but a phone or video meeting could work well too. Ask each to rate their fundraising participation for the prior year. Ask what worked and what didn't. Inquire about training that could help increase their involvement. Let each know you are available to partner and support their efforts. Ask each to recommit for the coming year. If your board doesn't use a fundraising commitment form, now is the time to introduce this. Most likely there will be resistance. That is a good thing — you want to grow into a board where members are proud to give and fundraise.

Introducing a formal commitment form can start a catalytic conversation.

If you are the chair of the board development committee: Meet with members to assess your commitment as a committee, and to assess the board's commitment to fundraising. What is working? What strategies or activities were most successful? Are there problem areas that impede fundraising? What needs to be addressed in the new year for the board to take on a larger role in fundraising? Is there a specific project or fundraising priority the board can take on? If the board is not yet a "fundraising board," what activity can be introduced to move in that direction? Don't be afraid to set a specific amount as a goal. A defined goal (with a timeframe) allows you to measure progress. Be sure to measure!

If you are the CEO of a nonprofit or the president of a college: Commit to your role as the chief fundraising officer. You may have a development director or even an advancement department, but at the end of the day you are the person responsible for the organization's or institution's bottom line. Review your calendar and make time for cultivation and solicitation activities with potential major donors and supporters. Schedule time to meet with your top fundraising/development person. Ask "what do you need to be successful," listen to the response, and work together toward success. Set your own fundraising goal. Determine how much you will personally raise in the coming year and secure the involvement of those who can help you reach that goal.

Your commitment will show up on the bottom line!

First published January 12, 2015.

Tips to Achieving Fundraising Success

If you are lucky, you are fortunate to know people who are the real deal. That is Lisa Hoffman. She is an experienced and talented fundraiser and coach. An expert who is both gentle and firm in her guidance, her goal is to help you reach your fundraising goals.

We recently reached out to Hoffman and asked her to share some of what she has learned during her 30 years in fundraising. We began by asking about what exactly leads to fundraising success.

"Board leadership really is essential," Hoffman began. "The board chair needs to give generously and raise money, as well as understand their role in modeling, guiding, and supporting the rest of the board to do the same. The board chair has tremendous influence on creating a culture of philanthropy, generosity, and giving. And if there are issues with board members, it is usually the chair who needs to step up and address them."

"The executive director or CEO needs to be one of the organization's lead fundraisers and partner with the board chair on keeping fund development high on the board's agenda and radar," she said. "Another critical part of the executive's role is to create a culture of generosity and appreciation of the individuals and groups that support the organization. Every staff member can be a leader in raising money, recruiting volunteers, and garnering in-kind contributions. The executive sets the tone and process for this kind of engagement."

"Passion is critical to successful fund development," she said. Most people don't like fundraising, and passion for their organization's mission is the best motivator I know of to provide the drive and fearlessness needed to raise game-changing amounts of money over the long haul."

"A plan is another key component," Hoffman added. "Our colleague Jude Kaye says that, 'A vision without a plan is hallucination.' I agree with her perspective. Fund development, without a plan that includes mission, vision, goals, and a roadmap for success, flounders."

Related to leadership, we asked Hoffman to share what she has identified as the qualities to look for in a board chair.

"A board chair should have clarity about the role and what leadership means — to support and drive the board in stewarding the organization's mission and vision. That means making sure every board member understands and fulfills their role in ensuring that every aspect of the organization — how people are treated, strategic direction, finances, fundraising — reflect sound values and respect the time and resources given to the organization," she shared.

"Also, courage to deal with issues that typically range from financial challenges to founder executive director succession to troublesome board members with integrity and skill," she said. And lastly, "A good sense of humor — which I think is self-explanatory!"

First published September 28, 2015.

Three Powerful Fundraising Tools

Every time we work with an organization, agency, or college we experience a feeling of deep connection with the people gathered at the table. Whether presenting information, listening to concerns, or developing strategies, we are also meeting new friends. We are witnessing diverse individuals put their beliefs into action, and we are inspired. Nonprofit board members and volunteers are some of the best people we will ever meet. They are passionate, knowledgeable, experienced, well-connected, thoughtful, and resourceful. And, we know that you — our readers — share these qualities.

Whether we have met you or not, you energize us and encourage us. We write this column each week to provide you with information that can help you meet the challenges and take advantage of opportunities.

If you are a frequent reader you know there is no magic wand that will ensure your organization has all the resources needed to sustain and grow. But there are ways you can increase the effectiveness of your board and increase the number of donors and funders who support your work.

We have written three additional books that can help you grow your nonprofit's fundraising. They are at the core of all our work and they inform our column FUNdraising Good Times on a weekly basis. See if one of these additional books is right for you and your nonprofit.

Prerequisites for Fundraising Success walks you through the steps for planning, launching, and maintaining successful fundraising programs. You will learn how to set attainable goals, develop a fundraising plan, hire the right staff, encourage teamwork, and tell your story and raise awareness. Other topics include recruiting volunteers and cultivating leaders, approaching donors, managing your data, and rewarding donors.

The Fundraiser's Guide for Soliciting Gifts is ideal if you have been asked to raise money but are not sure how to proceed. You will learn how to prepare to meet with a prospective donor, what to say and do when meeting with a donor, exactly how to ask for a gift, what to do when a donor says "Yes," what to do when a donor says "No," and how to close a meeting with a potential donor or funder.

FUNdraising Good Times Classics, Volume 1 is a collection of our best strategies for fundraising professionals, volunteers, and nonprofit leaders. Topics covered include feasibility studies, proposal writing, marketing, soliciting gifts, special events, board development, strategic planning, fundraising ethics, and career advice.

All three books are available from Amazon.com.

About the Authors

Mel Shaw and Pearl Shaw are the founders of Saad&Shaw – Comprehensive Fund Development Services.

Saad&Shaw provides clients with a unique brand of fundraising that combines marketing, corporate partnerships, and the best of business leadership with fundraising fundamentals. The firm is known for designing innovative fundraising programs that increase revenue, strengthen partnerships, and provide value to all parties. Core services include campaign research, planning, design, and implementation. Clients include colleges and universities, health care institutions, grassroots groups, and philanthropy organizations.

The concepts and strategies employed by Saad&Shaw are based on the 60 years of combined experience of principals Melvin and Pearl Shaw. In 2008 the Ford Foundation asked Mel and Pearl to share their unique brand of fundraising with social justice foundations from around the world at a conference held in Cartagena, Columbia, in South America. More recently they have been asked by The Assisi Foundation of Memphis, Inc. to provide fundraising technical assistance to regional nonprofits.

Saad&Shaw are proud to offer one of the most experienced, innovative, and creative powerhouse partnerships in fundraising consultancy today.

Melvin B. Shaw, Ph.D. *honoris causa*, is the founder of Saad&Shaw and serves as vice president of creative and strategy. He offers more than 50 years of experience in fund development and marketing. Formerly the vice president of marketing for the United Negro College Fund (UNCF), he created and produced the Lou Rawls Parade of Stars Telethon, raising $4 million annually in corporate sponsorships and more than $500 million in annual gifts to date.

Mel also served as the executive director of the Texas Association of Developing Colleges, facilitating joint programs and fundraising. He is nationally recognized for his work in creating and designing programs that combine marketing and fundraising and increase revenue and alumni/volunteer engagement. Mel's strategies create involvement and opportunities for corporate partnerships. He has developed cause marketing programs for Anheuser-Busch, General Motors, American Airlines, Chrysler Black Dealers Association, McDonald's, Essence Magazine, Disney World, and 7-Eleven, and worked on the feasibility study for the National Museum of African American History and Culture, a Smithsonian Institution Museum.

Prior to forming Saad&Shaw Comprehensive Fund Development Services, he headed his own firm, Shaw & Company, which specialized in capital campaigns, annual giving, development assessments, feasibility studies, board development, campaign designs and planning, and major donors. Mel holds a Bachelor of Science degree from Lane College in Tennessee; a master's degree in business education from the University of Memphis; and was a fellow at Harvard University's Institute of Educational Management. In 1991 Mel received an honorary doctor of humanities degree from Lane College in recognition of his unique donor engagement and cause marketing programs and their impact on the fields of philanthropy and higher education.

Pearl D. Shaw, CFRE, is a fund development strategist and nationally syndicated writer with management experience in the private and non-profit sectors. As the president of Saad&Shaw, she works directly with diverse nonprofit and higher education leaders conducting feasibility studies, designing fundraising programs, and leading training sessions that engage trustees, volunteers, and staff.

Prior to forming Saad&Shaw she headed her own firm, Phrased Write, providing nonprofit organizations with proposal writing, executive coaching, and strategic fund development services. She has also served as development director of the Women's Funding Network, an international association of more than 150 women and girls' foundations, and as a major gifts officer for Mills College. Her private-sector experience includes operations management, business development, and marketing for a software development firm. As a principal at Saad&Shaw she works directly with diverse nonprofit leaders conducting feasibility studies, designing fundraising programs, and conducting fundraising training sessions that engage trustees, volunteers, and staff.

Pearl serves on the board of the Tennessee Education Lottery Corporation. She is a member of the Association of Fundraising Professionals (AFP), and the marketing committee of the Women's Foundation for a Greater Memphis. She holds a B.A. from the University of California at Berkeley, and a Master of Public Administration degree from California State University East Bay. She is a Certified Fundraising Executive (CFRE) and a graduate of the Leadership Memphis class of 2012.

counselOnDEMAND

Let Saad&Shaw help you meet your fundraising challenges and manage your fund development resources and staff effectively. The firm's counselOnDEMAND service provides flexible, low-cost fund development coaching and strategy sessions for executives and development directors. Clients receive five hours of on-call expertise each month. This service can be used for proposal and document reviews, strategy sessions, coaching and mentoring, the development of a fundraising plan, and more. counselOnDEMAND is ideal for organizations with limited budgets. For others it can be the first step in preparing for a feasibility study, the creation of a campaign plan, or as a follow-up service for continuing clients. Contact Saad&Shaw by emailing info@saadandshaw.com or calling (901) 522-8727.

Learn More
To learn more about Saad&Shaw, including services, fundraising tips, and testimonials, visit saadandshaw.com.

Read Saad&Shaw's FUNdraising Good Times blog at saadandshaw.com/blog.

Other books by Mel Shaw and Pearl Shaw:

Prerequisites for Fundraising Success: 18 Things Every Fundraising Professional, Board Member, or Volunteer Needs to Know.

The Fundraiser's Guide to Soliciting Gifts: Turning Prospects into Donors

FUNdraising Good Times Classics: A Collection of Nonprofit Advice Columns, Vol. 1

The Grand Experiment

All books are available at Amazon.com.